52 Ways
To Re-connect,
Follow Up, &
Stay in Touch . . .

When You Don't
Have Time To Network

Anne Baber & Lynne Waymon

KENDALL/HUNT PUBLISHING COMPANY
4050 Westmark Drive   P.O. Box 1840   Dubuque, Iowa 52004-1840

52 Ways To Re-connect, Follow Up, & Stay In Touch ... When You Don't Have Time To Network may be purchased in quantity from the authors by corporations, associations, and other organizations.

Write

Waymon & Associates
622 Ritchie Ave.
Silver Spring, MD 20910
301-589-8633

Or call

1-800-352-2939.

Baber, Anne, 1938-
  52 Ways To Re-connect, Follow Up, & Stay In Touch ... When You Don't Have Time To Network / Anne Baber and Lynne Waymon.— 1st ed.
  ISBN 0-8403-9224-9
  1. Business communication. 2. Careers. 3. Interpersonal communication. I. Waymon, Lynne. II. Title.

Thanks . . .

To Jamie and thousands of other people in corporations and associations, nationwide, who came to our Great
Connections workshops and said, *"Okay, I understand
now how to meet people, but how do I keep that connection
going when I don't have **time** to network?"*

This book's for you.

Contents

What's the Problem?

"To me, the problem is that I go to a networking event and meet a lot of people and then — nothing happens. What am I doing wrong?"
— Mike, CPA

"I talked to her at last month's meeting, but I can't figure out what to do next. If I don't do something pretty soon, she'll forget who I am and what we talked about."
— Nancy, franchise owner

"I know I should stay in touch with past clients, but I don't know what to say when I call."
— Roger, freelance designer

"Bob's business is similar to mine, and I'm sure I could learn a lot from him. Come to think of it, we're doing some advertising that he'd probably like to know about, but I'm not sure what the next step is."
— Susan, sales rep

Mike, Nancy, Roger, and Susan are typical of networkers everywhere. They're trying to figure out how to re-connect, follow up, and stay in touch. And how to fit this relationship building into their already overloaded lives.

All too often, networkers — even rather savvy ones — don't follow up systematically. They spend lots of energy making initial contacts — and then don't know how to cultivate them so that the relationships pay dividends down the road.

They need advanced techniques that will help them build and maintain business connections — mutually beneficial ones — for the long term.

That's what this book is all about.

If your networking isn't paying off, **your** problem may be that you are not following through. The ideas in this book - one for every week in the year - will help you do just that . . . easily, comfortably, professionally.

Rate Your Relationships

How does your network rate? Here's a quiz to help you determine the value of your networking relationships. Jot down the names of 10 networking contacts, then use the quiz to rate each relationship separately, beginning with number one on your list.

Instructions

Circle Y for Yes if you agree with the comment; circle N for No if you cannot agree with the comment.

My networking contact

Y N 1. Recognizes my name instantly when I call.

Y N 2. Knows me well enough to recognize me "out of context," at the store, in a new group.

Y N 3. Demonstrates knowing my face **and** my name by coming up to me in a crowd and saying hello and by introducing me accurately to others.

Y N 4. Has my phone number handy in his/her address book or Rolodex™.

Y N 5. Knows the name of my company and where it is located so well that he/she could give people directions to it.

Y N 6. Can describe accurately what I do.

Y N 7. Gives vivid examples of what I do.

Y N 8. Knows that I am good at what I do and can cite reasons why my service or product is superior.

Y N 9. Knows of some independent verification of my expertise - an award, certification, third party endorsement.

Y N 10. Regularly sends me valuable information and resources.

Y N 11. Responds to requests from me.

Y N 12. Knows what kind of customers or clients my products or services will appeal to and is on the lookout for those people.

Y N 13. Always speaks well of me to other people and passes my name around.

Y N 14. Regularly refers qualified customers or clients to me.

Y N 15. Consistently creates opportunities to stay in touch with me.

Scoring Yourself

Add the number of Ys you circled for each person and see the comment below that corresponds with that number.

1 - 4	You do not yet have a viable networking relationship with this contact. Use the ideas in this book to create a strong, mutually beneficial relationship.
5 - 8	Your contact should know a lot more about you so he/she can provide better support for you. Teach your contact who you are and what you need and want.
9 - 12	Your contact is on the verge of becoming really valuable to you and already is providing quite a bit of assistance. Analyze your responses on the quiz and determine areas to strengthen in the relationship
13 - 15	You should be reaping the bottom-line benefits of networking. Your relationship with your contact is solid. Now, work on maintaining that relationship. Use the ideas in this book to refresh and renew the relationship regularly.

As another check on the quality of your networking relationships, imagine that your contacts are rating you. What score would they give you? What do you need to do to make the relationships with your contacts more valuable to them?

4

 sk not only what your contact can do for you, but what you can do for your contact.

The Five Goals of Follow Up

Hoping that something will come of your networking efforts is not enough. You must know exactly what you're trying to achieve as you create networking relationships. The quiz you just took provides many clues about what makes a valuable relationship. Aim for these the five goals as you re-connect, follow up, and stay in touch.

As you develop the relationship, make sure your contacts:

1. Know your name and how to reach you easily.
2. Understand exactly what you do.
3. Develop faith in your ability to serve or supply them — or people they refer to you — expertly.
4. Know what kinds of clients or customers you are seeking and are ready to refer them to you.
5. Understand what kind of information you need and are ready to help you find it.

As you reach these goals with your contacts, you will begin — and continue — to reap the benefits of networking. If your contact is a client or customer, staying in touch will encourage repeat business and referrals.

The Magic Number

Can you fit following up into your already jam-packed life? Sure. The magic number is 52. If you try just one of the *52 Ways* each week of the year, you'll be amazed at how quickly your networking efforts will begin to pay off.

Start now. Use the *52 Ways* in any order you like. Pick one and follow up -- effectively. As you deepen and strengthen your networking relationships, you and your contacts will exchange more and more valuable information.

Researchers have documented the bottom-line benefits of effective follow up. In one organization that provides networking clubs, members reported an average of a 20 percent increase in business -- but only after they had been members for a year. In another organization, the dollar value of referrals leaped up from $250 to more than $5,000 -- but again, only after members had been together for more than a year.

The Reciprocity Principle:
Give and you will get more than
you gave.

Networking in a Nutshell

Most people think they know what networking is all about. But, based on our experience with thousands of workshop participants, we believe that people have a multitude of misconceptions about networking.

It's not about using people. It is about relating to people in a way that's mutually beneficial.

It's not a numbers game in which you hand out your business card to everyone who crosses your path. That's only a cardboard connection. It is about carefully nurturing a selected group of people who can contribute to your success and to whose success you can contribute equally.

It's not an event. It is a process. Like all relationships, networking relationships must be created step by step.

It's not something you can buy as you plunk down your dues to belong to a networking group. You must take responsibility for building your network. No one else can do it for you.

It's not merely appearing. It is about interacting.

It's not something you do only when you are job hunting. It is vital to your career success. No matter what your career situation, you can — and should — network.

It's not instantaneous. It does take time and effort. You can't start today and have a valuable network tomorrow

There are four stages people go through as they begin to network.

*B*eginning networkers usually focus on "What's in it for me." But that's only part of the story.

Stage One: Taking

Networking is not just about taking. Most people who begin to network focus, at least initially, on trying to get something for themselves. There's nothing wrong with wanting your efforts to pay off. But, that's only part of the story.

Sometimes the Taking approach pays off. It works when you happen to connect with somebody who has what you want or needs what you're offering. But more often than not, it's no more than a face-to-face cold call. If you are focusing only on taking, your "prospect" may feel used.

The best networkers approach the process with the opposite point of view. They give more than they get — every day. Look back at the quiz and think about how your contacts would rate you. To benefit from networking, be a valuable contact for others. That's how you can plug into the Reciprocity Principle: If you give somebody something, he or she will try to give you something back. In fact, researchers who have confirmed this quirk of human nature say that, not only will the person you've given to try to pay you back, that person will insist on giving you more than you gave!

*O*ne-time trades don't necessarily create a networking relationship.

Stage Two: Trading

The point of networking is to exchange something of value. Trades accomplish that. But, networking is not just about trading — giving and getting — as important as that is. Trades are exciting. They make you feel as if your networking efforts are worthwhile. They pay off instantly. But again, that's only part of the story.

JoAnn, who has her own training company, went to a networking breakfast and met Peter, who has a window-washing business. She was delighted because she needed that service — right now. She took Peter's card so she could call him and get an estimate. He took her card because he knew his boss was looking for someone to write a training manual. That's a great trade. But it's a one-time trade and probably not the beginning of a long-term networking relationship — unless both parties work at creating one.

What happens in the Taking and Trading stages usually produces Single-sale Networking. Though Single-sale Networking may result in instant gratification, it's time consuming, and you miss out on the long-term benefits. Unfortunately, many people feel that, when they have reached the trading stage, they've reached the epitomé of networking.

But, you can have more.

s important as WHAT you know and WHO you know is WHO KNOWS YOU.

Stage Three: Teaching

A long-term, networking relationship is built by teaching other people what you need — and learning what they need. When you meet someone, take the time to be interested in that person and his or her business. Put your antenna up for resources, ideas, tips, information, or access that you could give to that contact. Look for ways to become known to that person, to educate that person about yourself and your capabilities. We call this kind of networking Relationship Networking.

If JoAnn teaches Peter what kind of clients or customers she is looking for, then Peter may send some her way. Or, if JoAnn teaches Peter what kind of information she's looking for, perhaps Peter can direct her to that resource or to someone who has that information.

Remember the old line: "It's not what you know, it's who you know"? Not true. **What** you know **is** important. It's your expertise, your knowledge, what you get paid for. **Who** you know is important, too. Those are the people you call when you are looking for an idea, a resource, a referral.

But more important than what you know and who you know is **WHO KNOWS YOU**. Networking is about making **WHO KNOWS YOU** as important as what you know and who you know.

You don't have a networking relationship until your contact knows you so well that, when an opportunity comes by that you would benefit from, your contact says,

"*I've got to call Jim about that!*"

or

"*I'll just mail this to Karen.*"

A networking relationship means somebody (besides you!) is looking out for your best interests while you look out for theirs. One big networking challenge is how to teach your contacts who you are and what you are looking for, so they can send good things your way. An equally big challenge is how to learn about your contacts and what they are looking for, so you can send good things **their** way. That's the way to make sure your contacts' "antennas" are up for you, listening for and alert to opportunities for you. Make sure you spend as much time learning your contact's business as you do teaching him or her what you do.

Many of the *52 Ways* help you to teach and to learn.

*N*etworking relationships become most valuable when you reach the Trusting stage.

Stage Four: Trusting

One more thing is necessary to make the relationship even more valuable and viable — trust.

Ultimately, Relationship Networking is about developing trust. If Peter doesn't show up to clean JoAnn's windows when he says he will or if he doesn't do a good job, JoAnn won't recommend him to her friends and acquaintances. On the other hand, if he is reliable, appears when he says he will, prices his service reasonably, and leaves her windows sparkling clean, then JoAnn will pass his name around enthusiastically. At the same time JoAnn teaches Peter about what she needs, she must also teach him to trust her or he will not be willing to give her name to people or to help her find what she's looking for.

As you think about networking, think about how you and your contacts can move beyond Taking and Trading to Teaching and ultimately Trusting each other.

When you get to mutual trust, networking relationships pay off big — for both parties.

*N*etworking is not
a numbers game.

Your Contacts

One of the biggest mistakes networkers make is to think networking is a numbers game. They go to networking events and hand out business cards to everyone they meet. That's not very effective. In fact, it's often a waste of valuable time. It should be obvious to you that you can't have the kind of intense networking relationships we are describing with hundreds of people. So choose your contacts carefully. Select people whom you can help as much as they can help you.

If you are in sales or in business for yourself, build your network to boost sales and put you in touch with valuable business resources.

If you provide professional services, develop contacts that can bring you a steady stream of referred— and qualified — clients or customers.

If you are in the process of changing careers or looking for a job, include more people in your network and be specific about how they can help.

If you have a job, create a network at work to help you get your job done better and easier. And, to protect you in case your job doesn't last forever, create a network beyond work.

Your network will never be "complete" or "in place." It will always be changing as you develop new contacts and renew or refresh existing contacts and allow previous contacts to go dormant. It's a journey, not a destination. So, enjoy the trip!

The Trust Factor

Gladhand networking doesn't work because giving people a business card does not establish trust. We only trust people when we have been assured of — or experience — their

- Character and
- Competence.

Their trust in us is also based on these two elements.

The Trust Matrix

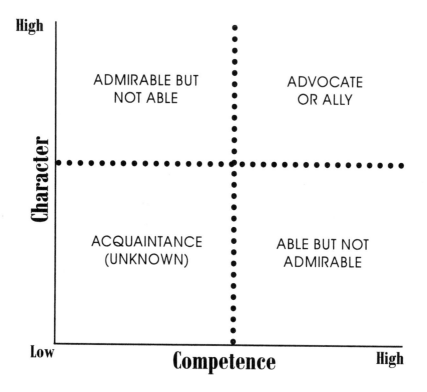

Demonstrate Your Character

You can teach people to trust you by demonstrating your **character** as the relationship progresses.

- Do what you say you will do.
- Be fair and honest.
- Be professional.
- Keep commitments — be on time and reliable.
- Keep confidences.
- Speak well of other people.
- When things go wrong, make them right immediately.
- Say, upfront, what you want.
- Give more than you get.

Demonstrate Your Competence

You also can teach people to trust you by demonstrating your **competence** as the relationship progresses.

- Do an excellent job.
- Become a recognized expert.
- Tell success stories when people ask you, "What's new?"
- Ask your satisfied customers or clients to provide testimonials.
- Take on a visible role in an organization — a role that showcases your capabilities.
- Speak to organizations or write an article for the newsletter or magazine.
- Provide a sample or demonstration.
- Get an advanced degree or professional credential.
- Win awards.
- Give more than you get.

You sell not only what you
make but who you are.

When you meet someone, you probably have little knowledge of that person's competence and character. And, your contact probably doesn't know you either. That's why most relationships begin in the lower left quadrant of The Trust Matrix with competence and character still to be determined. You are Acquaintances.

If a contact has a "bad experience" with you -- or if you have a "bad experience" with your contact -- your relationship will derail into the upper left quadrant or the lower right quadrant.

If your relationship ends up in the upper left quadrant, your contact trusts your character, but questions your competence. You are Admirable But Not Able. This situation can be remedied. It could be that you have just changed jobs or just graduated and are in your first job or have moved into a new career field. Look at the *52 Ways* to find out how to teach your contact about your success. Tell success stories as you talk or send out a newsletter or press release to let contacts know about your increasing expertise. Take a visible role in organizations, so contacts can experience your competence first hand.

If your relationship moves to the lower right quadrant, your contact trusts your competence, but questions your character. Your contact believes you are Able But Not Admirable. This is a difficult mindset to change. You will have to demonstrate repeatedly that your character is admirable.

If you have positive experiences with each other, your networking relationship will move to the top right quadrant. You will become Advocates or Allies. Advocates speak well of you and your business, refer qualified customers or clients to you and create opportunities for you. Allies are trusted advisors. Your trust in the confidentiality of the relationship and the value of the relationship is so high that you share frustrations, trade secrets, and successes. Developing this kind of trust takes time.

It's also possible that one of you — or both of you — may have established a reputation in the community. Ideally, you want contacts to hear good things **about** you before they hear **from** you. If your good reputations precede you, your relationship may start off in the upper right hand quadrant. If so, you've "jump started" the process and begin your relationship with character and competence assumed.

Once your relationship is established, however, continue to re-affirm both character and competence and refresh the relationship regularly.

As you re-connect, follow up, and stay in touch, you will be investing in the net worth of your network.

Reasons to Re-connect

The *52* **Ways** will give you good methods for re-connecting — even if you've only met your contact once. But many networkers still feel uncomfortable about taking that first step to re-establish a dialogue.

You can, of course, suggest another meeting when you first meet someone. In that case, you might say, *"I'd like to talk with you more about that. May I give you a call next week to set up a time to get together?"*

If you did not say something like that when you met, you may never see that person again. You have a good reason to re-connect — you'd like to build a relationship. But that may feel like too much to ask for initially. People tell us they'd feel more comfortable if they had "an excuse" for calling or setting up another encounter.

We call these "excuses" re-openers because they re-open a conversation by reminding your contact of something you have in common. After re-opening the conversation, the next step is to say, *"Let's get together."* Use the *52* **Ways** to get ideas about your next encounter.

Re-openers

- Refer back to when and how you met.
  "We both took that computer course a couple of weeks ago. I started using one of the software packages they suggested. How about lunch sometime next week? I'll tell you about it."

- Refer to a common need.
  "Since we are both starting businesses, I was interested in what you said about looking for office space. I'm working on that, too. How about getting together to talk about strategy?"

- Refer to proximity.
  "We work near each other, let's get together for lunch."
  "We live in same neighborhood, let's meet at the deli for supper next week."
  "We sat at the same table at the Chamber of Commerce dinner. I'd like to know more about your Total Quality Management program that you were telling me about."
  "I enjoyed talking with you when we sat next to each other at the committee meeting last week. I'd like to know more about your business. How about if I pick you up for this week's meeting and we can talk on the way?"

- Refer to a common background.
  "I noticed that we both went to the University of Florida. I got a flyer saying there is going to be an alumni get-together to watch the game next week. Would you like to go?"
  "Don't you have a degree in English, too? I'd be very interested to know how you made the transition to PR. How about meeting me for coffee later this week?"

- Appreciate your contact's contributions.

  "I thought your newsletter article was very interesting. I'd like to hear more about the task force you're involved in. How about lunch?"

  "You're doing a great job heading up the program committee. I did that for the Des Moines chapter, and I know what a big job it is. We developed a great checklist for planning any event. If you think your committee members could use it, I'll drop it by your office."

- Refer to a common acquaintance

  "You know Burt Johanes, don't you? He suggested we get together. I'm heading up the fund raiser for the hospital and he said you did one last year and might give me some pointers. How about breakfast next week?"

- Refer to time or money savers.

  "I heard you say that you are feeling overwhelmed with paperwork. I used the services of an office organizer. I'd be happy to share some of her tips for overhauling an office. Would you like to come over to my office late Tuesday afternoon?"

*H*i! How are you?"
"Not bad. How are you""
"Pretty good. What's new?"
"Not much. What's new with you?"
"Not much. Well, it's great to see you."
"Yeah. Good to see you. Let's get together sometime."
"Sounds good. See you."

Making Encounters Count

Make every encounter with your contact count. Don't get trapped in dead end conversations like the one on the opposite page.

Telling Success Stories

Since your contact can't always be there to see you in action, demonstrate your character and competence by telling success stories. These are short, punchy anecdotes in which you tell how you succeeded. When a contact asks you, "What's new?" tell a story that includes a reference to some aspect of your character or competence.

When a contact asked Carrie, who has her own PR business,"What's new?" Carrie said, "I was really scrambling yesterday. I had been working with an artist on a brochure for Oak Tree Mall and her office was flooded after all this rain we've been having. So, to get the artwork done on schedule, I helped her find a colleague whose computer she could borrow for the afternoon. She finished the artwork, and we got the layout to the client on the deadline as we had promised. Boy, was he happy!"

A story like this does several things. It positions you as having a prestigious client — Oak Tree Mall, providing a third-party endorsement. It verifies that you will go to heroic lengths to meet your deadlines. It mentions a satisfied client. And, most of all, it gives your contact a concrete picture of exactly what you do.

During your encounter, spend an equal amount of time learning about your contact's character and competence. Ask your contact for stories. Use questions like these:

"What have you been working on lately?"
"Tell me about the last project you completed."
"What's your next project?"

When Louis asked Kathleen, a CPA," *What's new with you?"* She said, *"One of my clients received a penalty for underpayment of taxes. I wrote a great letter to the Kansas Department of Revenue about the situation. They agreed with me and removed the penalty. My client was very pleased."*

As trust develops, your relationship will begin to pay off with important information, valuable resources, bigger leads and referrals, and opportunities for both of you.

Creating an Agenda

Before you meet, write out your Agenda so that your conversation helps you develop the relationship and doesn't wander off into chitchat and clichés. Everybody's Agenda has two parts: What You Have To Give and What You Want To Get.

Always be prepared to give your contact something. By giving, you tap into the Reciprocity Principle and encourage your contact to look for ways to give you something back.

Your "To Give" List

On your "To Give" list include

Enthusiasms What are you so excited and enthusiastic about that you'd talk to anybody, anytime, anyplace about it? Perhaps, you take tap dancing or Country Western dancing lessons and can tell other people how to sign up. Perhaps you took your first ride in a glider, used a new conference center, took a course on negotiating. Share your enthusiasms.

Discoveries What have you discovered recently? What little fact have you run across that other people might like to know about? Say you discover, for example, that there are 9,000 paid speaking engagements in the U.S. every day. Don't you suppose anyone who does public speaking would like to know that? Tell other people about your discoveries.

Resources What resources can you provide? Can you lend a book or tape? Can you get your contact into a library of training materials at the Community College? Can you invite a contact to attend a meeting of an organization you belong to? Share your resources.

Expertise What expertise do you have that you could offer? Can you tell someone how you self-published your book? How you researched child care facilities? How you got a job in a foreign country? How you learned Japanese? How to set up a vacation house swap? Tell others how to do something.

Referrals/Leads Can you give your contact the name of your auto mechanic, your window washing service, your house cleaners, your dentist, your accountant, your desktop publishing service? Can you tell your contact about someone who is looking for the product or service that he or she provides? Provide access to the right people.

Reviews Can you give people the name of a great Chinese restaurant? Your opinion of some new software? The name of a book you found useful or interesting? Help people find the best.

Ideas Can you give a trainer some new icebreakers for meetings? Can you provide new ideas on employee orientation programs that are working well in your organization? Can you suggest ways to handle business challenges or opportunities? Offer creative solutions, new perspectives.

Trends Can you tell people what's going on in your profession or industry? Can you pull together information from several sources and make a forecast? Provide insight into the future.

Support Without getting into an "Ain't it awful" conversation, can you express empathy and ask people if they'd like to hear what you did in a similar situation or if they'd like to brainstorm solutions, or if they'd like the name of an expert who might help them? Give a helping hand.

Shortcuts/Tips Can you pass along how you organized your office files? How you helped your sales force save time by creating a form for them to fill out, rather than requiring them to write reports? Help people save time or money or effort.

New Products/Services/Businesses Do you keep your eyes open for new items, services, or businesses? Can you pass along the name of a new mystery book store, a new consulting firm that specializes in helping companies make better decisions, an inexpensive place to buy office supplies? Tell people what's new.

The Trout-Fishing Rule

Notice that some of these suggestions for what you have to give to contacts involve non-business topics. That's because of the Trout-Fishing Rule. The Trout-Fishing Rule of networking says that you can make great connections when you talk about almost any subject — even about trout fishing. Any conversation will start the exchange of ideas and resources that build a relationship. Many business relationships start because trust is first established in a social setting or with a conversation about a topic that has nothing to do with work or business.

Your "To Get" List

The flip side of your Agenda is your list of What You Want To Get.

On your "To Get" list, include what you want to

Find What are you looking for? A networking organization to join? A new employee? A great location for your one-day spa business? A good place for your management meeting? A used photocopy machine?

Connect With Who are you looking for? An accountant? An interior designer? An office organizer? An exercise partner to take early morning walks with you?

Learn What skills or areas of expertise do you need to develop? How to evaluate bids from contractors who could do your office renovation? Public speaking? Your tennis game? How to improve the percentage of referrals you get from satisfied clients?

Understand What do you want to understand better? How various kinds of fax machines work? The pros and cons of contact management software programs? The "terrible twos?" Japanese culture and business practices? How house swapping works as an inexpensive way of vacationing?

Investigate What are you trying to research? Opportunities for franchise businesses? How people like working at home? Whether you should rent a post office box? Where to get disability insurance and how to decide what coverage you need?

Solve Are you facing a challenge or problem? Do you need ideas that will make your association's awards banquet really special? Entertainment for your son's seventh birthday party? Ways to encourage employees to take more responsibility? Ask your contacts for solutions.

Have More Of in Your Life More fun? More exercise? More time? More money? More friends? More balance? More vacations? More vegetarian restaurants?

A Word About Manipulation

Networking is not about manipulating other people. If you are absolutely honest about what you want to establish — a mutually beneficial, long-term, trusting, business relationship — you will not be manipulating your contacts. It's only when you try to get something for yourself through indirection, subterfuge, and telling only part of the truth that you are being manipulative. Don't do it. To build trust, you must convince your contact of your character, as well as your competence. Nothing destroys relationships quicker than manipulation. So, be totally upfront about what you have to give and ask appropriately for what you want to get.

*B*e upfront. Be honest. No mystery, no manipulation.

Using Your Agenda

What You Have To Give will grow and change every day. What You Want To Get is also ever-changing. Your various contacts — their interests and areas of expertise — also determine what kind of items you put on your Agenda for a meeting with them. So, create a new Agenda for each networking encounter. Always write your Agenda down and take it with you to your meeting or refer to it when you are on the phone with a contact.

Now, you are ready for a productive meeting. Help your contact focus on his or her Agenda, too. There are several ways you can do that:

- Teach your contact how to set an Agenda, using the suggestions above.
- Ask, "*How can I be helpful to you? What are you looking for that I might help you find?*"
- Listen generously. If your contact says, "*I'm planning my daughter's fourth birthday party.*" Don't just nod and say, "*That's nice.*" Say, "*I know of a clown who does birthday parties.*" Always be on the lookout for ways to be helpful.

Try making an Agenda. What do you Have To Give today?
What do you Want To Get today?

My Agenda

To Give	To Get

About the 52 Ways

These methods of reconnecting, following up, and staying in touch are the inventions of clever networkers around the U.S. When we found people whose networks really worked for them, we asked them, *"How do you follow through?"* Then, we field tested and refined the ideas in our workshops.

To help you choose methods that fit your personal goals, we've coded each of the **52 Ways**. The codes are described on the next few pages.

Some ways bring you face to face with people.

Some ways help you contact only one person. Others allow you to contact many people.

Some involve no extra time. Others require some extra time.

Some cost nothing. Some are relatively expensive.

Some take more time — or money, but reach a greater number of contacts. You'll have to take these kinds of tradeoffs into account. Balance the time or money each method takes with its potential for building the relationship.

The codes appear as equations, driving home the point that, as you invest time and money, you will make effective contact. Noticing these equations will help you decide which ways are right for you, with a particular contact in a particular situation.

Tip — Get Face to Face

*T*urner wrote a letter to his franchise training director recommending a speaker for the next training conference. Rather than call to say thanks, the speaker dropped by Turner's store. She said, *"Your letter was wonderful. I appreciated it so much. I will follow up with the training director. Do you have time to give me the grand tour and tell me about your products and services? I want to be able to recommend you to anyone I run into who needs printing."*

Faces

Face-to-face conversations are the most effective ways to build relationships. As you think about using the *52 Ways*, make every effort to figure out how you can turn a phone call into a face-to-face meeting. Remember that trust is best established face-to-face and that trust building takes time. To develop a networking relationship that meets The Five Goals of Follow Up will take six to eight face-to-face encounters, in addition to notes and phone calls.

Look for profiles of two people like the ones below in the top right hand corner of a page. If you see the profiles, that Way will bring you face-to-face with your contact. If you don't see any profiles, that Way of re-connecting relies on the written word or electronic communications rather than face-to-face contact.

Tip — Schedule It

L ouise plans to re-connect with 10 contacts each week. *"I know I won't take the time to keep up with people unless I put it in my planner,"* she says. *"So, every Friday, I make notes about who I'll call or meet during the next week. If I schedule my networking, it doesn't seem to take much time. If I'm going to attend a meeting, I call a contact and arrange to see that person — perhaps pick him up or sit next to her."*

Time

The title of this book promises that we'll help you find ways to connect that you can fit into your lifestyle. Yes, you can do networking on the run. You can use bits and pieces of time effectively. If you are going to be doing something anyway — eating lunch, attending a play, exercising — you can save time by turning that occasion into an opportunity to network. Set a goal for the number of networking calls and meetings you want to do every week. When you are planning your week, schedule your networking — just like everything else in your calendar that's important.

Along with each of the *52 Ways*, you'll see a quick code that will tell you at a glance whether that method will take Little or No Extra Time, Some Time, or Lots of Time.

Little or No Extra Time   **Some Time**   **Lots of Time**

Tip — Pay Your Way

*A*lways pay your fair share of the cost of networking. It's better to go "dutch treat" than to pay for a networking contact's meals, for example. Remember, you're trying to establish a mutually beneficial relationship. If one person always pays, the relationship also will become un-equal. You can't buy a networking contact. Most relationships work best when each person pays his or her way, not only with money, but with valuable information or referrals or resources.

Richard, a marketing consultant, called Mark, a printer, and asked him to lunch. When Richard grabbed the check, Mark said, *"Let's split this. That way, we won't have to try to remember whose turn it is to pay."*

Money

Most of the ways are free, but a few are costly. It's a trade off. Sometimes, you will decide that it's worth it to spend Some Money or Lots of Money to stay in touch with your networking contacts. Only you can make that decision.

Along with each of the **52 Ways**, you'll see a quick code - dollar signs - that will tell you at a glance whether that method will involve No Extra Money, Some Money, or Lots of Money.

Little or No Extra Money   **Some Money**   **Lots of Money**

Tip — Try Technology

*B*uy "contact management" software. It will help you keep track of details about contacts and make it easier to get in touch with small or large groups of people — everybody you know in Atlanta, people who are in sales, all the people who were customers last year. (For information on contact management software, see computer catalogs or contact a computer software salesperson.)

Bob sells speciality advertising and promotional items. When he calls contacts, his contact management software allows him to display the information he's collected about them on his computer screen, and he can update his files during every conversation. The software makes it easy to keep track of all kinds of information — both personal and business. *"Has twins," "Went to University of Missouri." "Planning 50th anniversary of company February 1994. Bought key chains in July 1993."*

People

Although meeting people face-to-face is the best way to develop networking relationships, sometimes it makes sense to contact many people.

Along with each of the *52* **Ways**, you'll see a quick code that will tell you at a glance whether you'll be able to use that method to keep in touch with One Person, Some People, or Lots of People.

One Person   **Some People**   **Lots of People**

Your Way

We encourage you to add to the list of *52* **Ways**. Ask your contacts how they stay in touch. Observe what works for other people. Always be looking for more ways to refresh and re-new and reinforce relationships. As you discover new meth-ods, tell us about them. To tell us about **Your Way**, use the form at the back of the book.

*N*etwork with competitors so you can refer business that's too small, too big, or too far away — or simply something you have no interest in doing.

1

Pass the Perks

Provide access to events, people, and resources — dinner with a visiting author, your library of training videos, a sneak preview of a movie, free tickets to an event.

Risa, a freelance writer, received a complimentary ticket from a neighborhood economic development organization to a business breakfast at the newly opened Australian Outback area at the zoo. Risa knew that the point of the event was to show off the renovated zoo to as many people as possible and to encourage business development in the neighborhood, so when she called to RSVP, she asked if she could bring an associate. Then, Risa called her contact Barbara, another freelancer, and said, *"How about joining me for breakfast in the Australian Outback?"* At the event, Barbara, who loved to write about animals, talked with the zoo's director about doing magazine articles on "the new zoo." That was a topic Risa wasn't interested in writing about.

*H*elp people
"see" what
you do.

2

Host a Meeting

Want to show some influential people where your business is located and give them a clear image of what you do? Offer your business as a meeting place for a committee or board. To make your business real to them, give a quick guided tour. Be ready to talk informally about awards on the wall, new equipment, new capabilities, and various services you provide.

*B*ill, an architect, followed up with Claire after she told him that the hospital fund-raising committee they were both serving on needed a place to meet. He offered the conference room at his office. At the committee meeting, Claire saw a photo collage of a school Bill's firm had just completed. *"I'll give your name to my brother-in-law,"* she said. *"He just bought a franchise child care business and has decided to build rather than renovate."*

*A*lways have interesting and valuable information to give your contacts.

3

Put Out a Newsletter

If your business involves providing information — and whose doesn't — produce a newsletter. Highlight your successes, new products and services. Show how clients or customers benefit. Help your contacts see how they could use your expertise. Create the newsletter yourself on your computer or find a freelancer who will do it for you.

*J*ohn designs office interiors. Every quarter he sends a newsletter to customers, potential clients, professional colleagues, and suppliers. His newsletter highlights new product information, news about recent clients, and interesting tidbits, tips, hints, and shortcuts. *"I get a lot of calls after people receive the newsletter,"* he says. *"And you know what people comment on the most? My Mission Impossible column that tells how we solved a difficult problem or met an impossible deadline. The newsletter generates both new and repeat business."*

E very chance meeting is an appointment. When you meet someone, try
to find out why you have an "appointment "
with that person.

4

Do a Lunch Bunch

Ask a few people you are trying to get to know better to lunch. Pick your lunch bunch carefully so that the benefits of their becoming better acquainted with you and each other are obvious. Or trust that any group of people will discover many common interests.

*M*arcella, who owns a small advertising agency, frequently invites a mix of clients and potential clients to a catered lunch in her conference room. *"They seem to enjoy meeting each other. Often, the stories my current clients tell to my potential clients 'sell' them on using my services."*

Don't let anyone tell you talk is cheap. Conversation can be your most important business asset.

5

Take a Guest

Invite your contact to a sports event, museum activity, or speech. Use your social activities to explore business possibilities in a relaxed setting.

Barbara, who has her own training business, noticed that season tickets to the university's theatre were only $25 — for 6 plays. She bought two tickets and enjoys inviting someone to join her. *"I like to catch up with six different contacts during the theatre season. It's a way to fit networking into my life,"* she points out.

*N*ever underestimate the
power of networking.

6

Send a Postcard

Out of town on business or vacation? Take some addresses with you. Buy a handful of postcards, or before you go, have postcards printed with your picture, your logo, a saying that makes people think of your service or product, or some interesting facts about your industry. Write notes telling about something you saw or did that your contacts would be interested in or use the note to confirm a future meeting with them.

O n vacation in Ft. Myers, Florida, Lewis, a graphic designer, sent postcards showing a photograph of Thomas Edison's home to a dozen contacts. He wrote: *"Enjoying my vacation. I just toured Edison's home. Isn't it interesting that we use the light bulb as a symbol for great idea?*

I hope you'll think of me when you need a 💡 for graphic design!"

T ake networking off your "To Do
List" and make it a way of life.

7

Travel Together

Going to a convention? Call a contact
well in advance and suggest that you
travel together.

*C*onnie and Fran have known each other for years as
members of The National Association for Female Executives. Making plans to attend the annual Network
Directors' Retreat, Connie called Fran and said, "*If you haven't
made your plane reservation yet, how about if we fly to the
convention together. It will be a good chance to catch up.*"

*N*ever go anywhere by yourself!
Take a contact along.

8

Share a Cab

Split the cab fare or ride the commuter train together to or from a meeting or event. You're going anyway. Why not make use of the time to get to know someone better?

*H*ank, who owns a printing franchise, and Ron, who owns an accounting and tax service franchise, met at the International Franchise Association Exposition. As they were standing in line to check out of the hotel, Hank asked Ron, *"Want to share a cab to the airport?"* On the way to the airport, he and Ron exchanged lots of valuable ideas about how to generate more sales by exhibiting at trade shows.

B uild your network be-
fore you need it.

9

Get Feedback

Ask your contact to review something you've written — brochure copy, your resumé, a newsletter article, a contest entry. Then call or visit to discuss your contact's comments. If you change anything about your materials as a result of the feedback, give a copy of the new piece to your contact pointing out how the comments helped you.

Tom joined a professional association. At the meeting, he asked everyone he met, *"Who should I talk to in my job search?"* Several people mentioned Margo, a past president and a person well-respected in the profession. So, Tom introduced himself and, after talking a while, asked if he could send her a copy of his resumé. She said *"Sure, but I don't know of any openings anywhere right now."* Along with his resumé, Tom sent Margo a self-addressed, stamped postcard and asked her to comment on his resumé. Because it was so easy to do, Margo returned the postcard with a couple of suggestions. Tom called her to thank her and then sent her the new version. Later, he followed up with a phone call. By that time, he'd built a relationship Margo, who eventually provided two job leads.

Y our network is created conversation by conversation, exchange by exchange, with the
people you meet every day, everywhere.

10

Message the Machine

Don't be discouraged if you reach someone's machine or answering service. Plan ahead to leave an effective, upbeat message. If you're caught off guard, hang up. Call back after you've worked out a well-organized and professional message.

*L*isa figured she might get Mark's voice mail when she called him, so she planned her message carefully before she dialed. She said, *"Hi, Mark. This is Lisa Montgomery. Just wanted to say thanks for telling me about the writers' conference. One book editor told me, 'It's easier to get a book published after you've been published in magazines.' So, I just sent my first article out to a magazine he suggested. Keep your fingers crossed for me, will you? And thanks again for tipping me off about the conference! I'll give you a call soon and tell you all about it."*

I nvest in the net worth
of your network.

11

Fax Timely Stuff

Fax time-sensitive information to your contact: an announcement about a professional meeting, a sale of computer equipment, a notice about a visiting author's book signing.

*L*orraine told Patrick about the video she was having produced and mentioned that she was looking for a supplier for the labels. *"I've got to get these labels done. . . fast," she said.* When Patrick received a paper catalog that offered video labels, he faxed Lorraine an order blank for the catalog with a note, *"Remembered your rush need for labels. Here's a source. Good luck with the video."*

***I**t's not the amount of time, but the quality of the interaction that counts in networking.*

12

Pull Up a Chair

At a meeting or event, plan to sit next to each other. Call your contact before the event to arrange to spend the time together.

Steve knew that unless he planned ahead he'd probably end up sitting with people he already knew at the monthly meeting of Sales Professionals International. He remembered talking briefly with Charles at last month's meeting and wanted to follow up with him about some sales training exercises he'd mentioned. So, Steve called Charles and said, *"How about saving me a seat at the meeting next Tuesday. I'd like to hear more about how you liked using those exercises."*

B e seriously curious.
Go beyond the super-
ficial.

13

Notice Publicity

Peruse the newspaper watching for publicity about your contact. Clip any mention and send a copy with a sticky note message. Or cut out your contact's advertisement and send with a note telling what made the ad leap off the page and grab your attention.

*A*l owns a landscape service. One of his customers said he wanted his lawn re-seeded because he was putting his house on the market. When Al found out his customer wanted to sell, he referred the customer to Connie, a realtor. Several weeks later, Connie, noticing Al's new ad about low-maintenance landscaping, clipped it and sent it to him with a note saying, "*This new ad really jumps off the page — especially the information about the low-maintenance shrubs. Bravo! I'll be sure to mention it to new homeowners.*"

*N*etworking creates "top-of-the-mind awareness." So, when your contacts see opportunities or information you could use, they will give it to you.

14

Announce Your News

Get the word out about an achievement, a move, a promotion. Send a news release, postcard, or note.

*K*ay, a career consultant, moved her office from her home to an office building. To announce the April move, she sent her contacts a package of seeds and a printed card that provided her new address and phone and said, *"We're growing, and you can too!"*

E xpert networkers teach who they are and what they have to offer.

15

Read All About It

Send your contacts an article that mentions you as an expert. If you haven't been in the news recently, send an article that gives information on the kind of service or product you provide. That way, you can "piggyback" on an article in the news media, positioning yourself as an expert.

*J*osh's firm analyzes overhead costs for small and mid-sized businesses. When The Wall Street Journal featured an article on rising overhead costs for small businesses, he sent copies, with a personal note and his brochure to 20 potential clients he'd met recently at networking events.

*M*ake your name memorable. When you introduce yourself, give people a tip to help them remember it.

16

Wish 'Em a Happy

Send a card on an unusual holiday —
Fourth of July, your birthday, Labor Day —
to avoid having your message become
just one of many at the end of the year.
Or send birthday cards to contacts on
their birthday.

Kathleen Murphy provides workshops and speeches for many organizations. She designed a St. Patrick's Day card to say thanks — and to encourage her contacts to *"Think Murphy"* when they need training.

*B*e a giver,
not a taker.

17

Throw a Party

Invite contacts to your place of business to give people a better idea of what you do. If you work at home, team up to find an interesting place for your open house. Select your co-host carefully. Look for someone with whom you might have customers in common.

*A*rtist Carol works at home, so she teamed up with frame shop owner Karl to showcase both businesses with an after hours wine and cheese party. She and Karl invited both past and potential customers to view Carol's drawings and see Karl's frames.

Y ou can do more than hope your networking efforts will pay off. You can make it happen.

18

Pass It On

When you discover a service or product you really like, promote it to others. People will thank you for introducing them to a great "find."

Dennis, a mortgage broker hired Caroline, a sales trainer, to work with his 16 sales people to improve their selling skills. Dennis was so pleased with the results that he held an open house for his friends, business contacts, and customers — all people who needed to improve **their** sales skills or their staff's skills. He invited Caroline to do a mini-session of her training. Three of Dennis's clients eventually contracted with Caroline to offer their junior salespeople a similar program — and they told Dennis how much they appreciated his tipping them off to Caroline's training expertise.

*B*y what we get, we make a living. By what we give, we make a life.

19

Give a Goodie

Send your contact a bagel and cream cheese or a couple of donuts — or even a single, specialty tea or coffee bag — along with some information you'd like that person to take time to look at. Notice that this technique "creates" time in your contact's day for him or her to focus on your information.

Paper sales rep Leslie found a gourmet grocer who delivers. She sends a surprise "coffee break" to current or potential customers — along with several paper samples for her contacts to look at while they enjoy the snack.

*A*lways give without remembering.
Always receive without forgetting.

20

Lend a Book

Deliver a book or audio tape you have enjoyed to a contact. If a brief visit is appropriate, ask about projects that person is working on and be ready to tell about your latest successes and challenges.

When Mike met Charles at a Rotary International luncheon, Charles said he'd like to read the latest Tom Peters' book, but that he was number 238 on the library's waiting list. Mike asked for his business card and said, *"I have a copy. I'll give you a call and bring it over to you as soon as I finish it."*

Your network will never be "finished;" it always will be evolving.

21

Sign Up a Volunteer

Many people people say they'd like to volunteer a little time to a good cause, but don't know what to do. Invite your contact to volunteer with you.

Wendie's final project for her graduate degree introduced 11-year-old girls to women with careers in scientific fields. Her project was designed to encourage the young girls to think about careers in science and to provide role models for them. She invited her contacts to take part in the project and enlisted their help to find additional women mentors for the girls. After the project was over, she invited the women to a dutch treat "Celebration Brunch" at a local restaurant to become better acquainted with them and to allow them to meet each other.

*N*o one else can create
your network for you.
You're in charge.

22

Tip Off the Talkers

Before a meeting begins, chat with the speaker or emcee. Let that person know what interests you about the topic and your experience with it. Presenters appreciate knowing more about their audiences. They may mention you from the podium, providing you with visibility, instant credibility, and endorsement by an expert or leader.

*F*red, owner of a franchise sign shop, showed up early at a workshop on marketing and talked to the speaker. She asked about his work and he said, *"I make all kinds of signs and banners for all kinds of businesses. I also do a complete range of signs that comply with Americans With Disabilities Act regulations."* When workshop participants moaned about how difficult it was to bring their business signage into compliance with ADA , the speaker said, *"Fred's company has exactly what you need. Fred stand up, so people will be able to find you during our coffee break."*

B e prepared to be spontaneous.
Plan ahead to give and get.

23

Get Re-introduced

Afraid the person you'd like to talk to again might not remember you? Ask a colleague or friend to re-introduce you.

Brian sells office phone systems. At a service club meeting three months ago, he'd introduced himself to Dave, who is in commercial real estate. At this month's meeting, Brian heard from a mutual acquaintance that Dave was looking for office space for a new client, a business relocating its corporate headquarters. Brian wanted to remind Dave about his phone systems, so he asked Mary to re-introduce him.

N ever hide your Agenda or try to manipulate others to get what you want. Be specific and honest about what you're looking for.

24

Profile Customers

Give your contacts a carefully thought out "profile" of your ideal customer or client and ask your contacts to mention you when one of those ideal folks crosses their path. Ask your contacts for their customer profiles, so you can reciprocate.

*K*evin, a certified financial planner, wants to remind his contacts how to identify people who might need his services. Kevin knows that people become more interested in financial planning when they are facing or have just been through significant life changes. When he meets with contacts, he hands out his "client profile" and asks them to pass his name along to people who are

- Getting married.
- Having a new baby.
- Celebrating their 30th, 40th, or 50th birthdays.
- Changing careers.
- Retiring.

*I*nformation is the new
business currency.

25

Create a Quiz

Design a quiz to "teach" people about your product or service. Put the quiz on a wallet-size card to give out to potential clients or print it larger to fax or mail. Make it short and eye-catching. If you are targeting older customers, make the print larger.

*J*eff, who owns a carpet store, created a quiz — "Do You Know How To Buy Carpet?" When he meets someone who is thinking about buying carpet, he says, "*Give me your business card, and I'll send you a copy of my quiz. It will help you know what to look for as you make your decision about buying new carpet. Of course, I hope you'll come by my store as you are shopping.*"

*B*uild relationships for the long term. Never assume you can use and discard people.

26

Provide a Calendar

Send your contact a calendar of events you'll be involved in or clients you will be working with. This idea works well for musicians, artists, trainers, consultants, craftspeople, speakers, freelancers, for example.

*A*lice imports fabrics and wearable art from Thailand. She sends contacts a postcard listing upcoming shows and craft fairs, with a note that says, *"Thanks for announcing this event to your friends last year. Looking forward to seeing you in May. Hope you'll pass the word to people you know who'd be interested in ALICE ART."*

Y our networking contacts won't
help you until they trust you.

27

Teach a Course

Teach a course at a community college or open university. Publicize the course to your contacts. Even if they don't take the course, letting them know you are teaching establishes your expertise.

*P*hotographer Sunita finds that, after she's taught a course, she always gets calls from several class members to do work in their organizations. She's delighted when her former students become her clients or refer clients to her. She believes the repeated contact with students over several months during the semester gives the relationships a chance to bloom. *"It's a matter of trust. My students get to know me and see what I can do,"* she says.

*G*reat networkers have pur-
poses; others have wishes.

28

Speak Out

Speak to the local chapter of an association and be sure the program planner publicizes your speech. Provide a news release for the program planner to send to the business calendar in your local newspaper.

*T*erry, a financial planner, worked on developing his speaking skills. Then, he told everyone he knew that he'd be delighted to speak at meetings on the topic, How To Finance Your Retirement. His speeches allow him to present his expertise to many people — and he always makes sure they go home with a brochure about his services.

H umorist Will Rogers said, "It ain't braggin' if you done it." Tell success stories.

29

Show Off

Showcase your expertise. If you are a
printer, print the organization's newsletter;
if you are an electrician, help with the
lighting for the summer theatre in the park
— and get your name in the program.

*R*ick is a consultant who specializes in strategic planning. He offered to conduct a free planning session for
the new board of directors of the community leadership group he belonged to. The planning session allowed him
to demonstrate his capabilities to a dozen members — the
new directors — who were executives in various businesses.
The planning session also provided a good opportunity for Rick
to get to know the executives in a relaxed setting during breaks
and over lunch.

*N*etworking is exchanging information and services in such a way that it builds the relationship.

30

Connect With a Card

Provide a card for your contacts to give to people. Make your business card a topic of conversation as well as a source of information. List products or services, include your picture, use a slogan, have it pre-cut to fit a Rolodex™, or design it to fold over, so it's a mini-brochure.

*L*ucia has two business cards. One is her corporate card, which gives her title — account executive — with a large telecommunications company and lists products and services she can provide. The other is bright blue and cut in the shape of a funny shoe. Anyone who sees her shoe card knows that Lucia is a clown. She gives her cards to contacts and asks them to pass her cards along to people who are having birthday parties or special events and might like to hire a clown to entertain.

P rofessional, community, service, and civic organizations give opportunities for making contact and developing relationships. But even better than that, getting active is a way to become visible.

31

Be a Winner

Enter awards programs — and win — to develop your reputation as an expert. After you collect your award, publicize the achievement in your association newsletter and local newspapers. You also can send a news release to your contacts.

Robert, president of a quality assurance consulting firm, encouraged his consulting team to enter the Quality Assurance Association's awards program. At the awards banquet, every consultant was recognized and other members of the association were encouraged to ask them about their project. *"Winning gave us 'the Good Housekeeping Seal of Approval,' not only with our peers in the association, but also with our clients and potential clients,"* Robert said. *"The credibility and expertise of each person on the team was enhanced."*

Work on the giving side of networking. You are in control of the giving side. You are not in control of the getting side.

32

Give a Prize

Become known for what you give away. Provide your product or service as a door prize at a meeting you are attending. Write out what you want the emcee to say about the prize — and you! That way, your donation will teach people what your business is all about and help them feel more comfortable striking up a conversation with you after the meeting.

*E*leanor, a career management counselor, offered one free hour of resumé review as the door prize at a professional meeting she attended. Several people who didn't win the prize, but wished they had, came over to ask Eleanor about her services.

*A*s you notice what kinds of help are most important to you, take every opportunity to help others the same way.

33

Link 'Em Up

When your contact needs a service or product, ask permission before you give his or her name to a supplier or salesperson. Then, call your resource person, provide the lead, and "take credit" for it. Call your contact several days later to be sure the connection has been made and that your contact is satisfied with the supplier or salesperson.

*A*t a networking breakfast, Naomi mentioned to Sid that she was in the market for a fax machine. Sid asked permission to have a supplier he knew call her. Naomi agreed. After the meeting, Sid called his supplier and said, "*I mentioned you to an acquaintance of mine — Naomi Hessler — this morning. She's looking for a fax machine. I've already raved about your excellent service. Just want you to know she's expecting a call from you. Here's her number.*"

*I*f you don't like the term "network-ing," call it "face-to-face marketing."

34

Offer a Ride

Look at your calendar for the next couple of weeks. What events are you going to? Could you offer a contact, whom you'd like to get to know better, a lift to a meeting?

S usan met Martha Lee at a Chamber of Commerce networking event. A couple of weeks later, Susan called her new contact and asked, *"Are you going to the Chamber's After Hours networking event this month? Why don't I swing by and pick you up? We didn't have much time to talk at the meeting. I'd love to hear more about your new business."*

*H*elp other people get what they want, and they will see to it that you get what you want.

35

Clip the News

As you skim newspapers or magazines, cut out articles of special interest to your contact and send the articles along with a personal note.

Deborah facilitated a team-building retreat for Hank's managers and hoped to provide several more workshops. But then, a mandate came down from Hank's home office: *"Put all of your people through Total Quality Management training by January 1."* And Deborah's workshops were on hold for nine months. To keep in touch, she sent Hank a couple of articles on team-building as a reminder of her expertise and interest.

J oining a networking organi- zation doesn't mean you join anybody's network — or that they join yours.

36

Haunt Their Habitats

Target your ideal clients. Describe those ideal clients/customers — including where you will find them. Once you identify their habitats, go there regularly, so that you have a setting in which you can begin to build long-term relationships.

*T*ran sells photographic papers and supplies. He discovered that 38 percent of the members of the local film society are photographers. So, he joined and became active in the film society to increase his opportunities for meeting and staying in touch with his target customers.

*T*ake notes after you talk with contacts, so you will remember to ask
how they liked the cruise or how their office renovation is coming along.

37

Brown Bag It

Set up a "brown bag" lunch with a speaker and invite your contacts to attend. Make sure the speaker is a an effective presenter and will talk about something that will interest your contacts.

*A*my, marketing director for a retirement complex, invited contacts — women over 45 — to a "brown bag" lunch at her facility. The speaker was a doctor on staff who talked about identifying Alzheimer's disease in aging parents.

*G*ive your contacts this book. To order extra copies, see the order form at the back.

38

Offer an Idea

Be on the lookout for ideas to give to your contacts. Listen generously to see how your fresh perspective or unique resources might help someone solve a problem. Creativity draws people toward you. If someone gives **you** an idea, acknowledge the giver. Close the loop and tell how you followed through with the suggestion. Let your contact know how the idea worked.

*T*alking with Kevin at a dog show, Martin mentioned that he'd like to take early retirement, but that he'd have to come up with some kind of business to make ends meet. Kevin heard about a successful new business in another city — U-Wash Puppy, a do-it yourself bathhouse for dogs. He called Martin, saying *"Heard about a new business in Omaha. Sounds like an interesting business opportunity that might be just as successful here in Tulsa."*

*A*ssume that your contacts have an Agenda — even though they may not realize it. Your job: Discover their Agendas.

39

Extend an Invitation

Want to see someone more frequently?
Encourage your contact to visit and perhaps join an organization you belong to.

Bill, who was leaving the military, met Eric at an alumni
function and told him he was interested in a new career in sales. Eric invited Bill to visit — and if he found it
useful, to join — the local chapter of Sales and Marketing Executives International as a way to explore career possibilities.

T ell your contacts how important they are to you.
Show your contacts how important they are to you by being
important to them.

40

Say Thanks

Be specific when you say thanks to your contact. Do it in person if at all possible.

S teve, who was job hunting, didn't limit his thanks to John to a general, "*Just wanted to say thanks to you for all you've done.*" Instead he said, "*John, I appreciate your sending me a list of organizations in Dallas that I might contact. It was very helpful to me to have 27 names to get in touch with. I'll let you know if some opportunities develop for me. Thanks again for your help.*" Later, after two of the calls resulted in interviews, Steve called John back to share the success.

Y ou're not networking until your contacts trust you to promote their success and believe you'll reward them for their efforts on your behalf.

41

Test Your Ideas

Ask contacts to participate in a focus group or test group to try out your ideas. Provide some sort of benefit to reward their participation, even if it's only a light supper.

Margo created patterns for crafts and sewing projects. Before marketing them, she asked former customers and potential customers to a "sewing bee" to be sure her instructions were crystal clear. Participants enjoyed the evening get-together and went home with a handcrafted item — and a very clear idea of what Margo does for a living.

L isten generously. Figure out how you can help your contact.

42

Bring People Together

At networking meetings and in other set-
tings, too, listen for commonalities so you
can introduce people to each other.

Susan takes the initiative to introduce people to each other, and they remember her as a great connector. She says, *"Chuck, I want to introduce you to Milt. He went to the University of Chicago, too."* Then, she moves on to talk with someone else: *"Darlene, I'm so glad to see you. You've got to meet Beverly. You've both started new businesses in the last year. I know you'll have a lot to talk about."*

H anding out your business cards to lots of people makes only "cardboard connec tions." To make a great connection, pour your energy into the conversation and look for a reason to give out your card.

43

Face It

Nothing succeeds like face-to-face contact — but that's not always possible. For
quick correspondence, get a notecard
(that fits in a business envelope) printed
up with your photo on it. Sending your
photo card when you need to communi-
cate puts your face in front of your contact.

A few days after the monthly Chamber of Commerce
mixer, Ron sends his photo card to several people he
met there. Often, he refers to something they talked
about. (Right after the event, he makes notes on the backs of
their business cards to jog his memory.) Sometimes, he just
writes, *"Hope to see you at next week's event."* Other times,
he provides information — a name and phone number, for
example — that he promised his contact he'd send along.
*"Using a notecard with my picture on it, means that people
come up to me at the next event to say hello. It really helps
them feel that they know me,"* he says.

*I*f we bestow a gift or favor and expect something in return, it is not a gift.

44

Scout for Talent

Suggest your contacts as speakers for service club meetings. Speaking allows your contacts to promote their businesses. Of course, you'll need to call them first to be sure public speaking is their idea of fun and to ask permission to pass their names along.

*K*im knew that her contact Christine was writing a book on personal courage. She remembered Christine saying, *"One thing that really helps me keep working on the book is to talk to groups about the ideas as I go along. That gives me deadlines."* After checking with her, Kim passed Christine's name along to the Women's Resource Network as a possible speaker.

*T*o see your contacts more frequently, invite them to join an organization you belong to — or create an organization.

45

Start a Club

Start a referral club, with only one of each type of business, whose only purpose is to refer leads to each other. Choose carefully to find club members with high competence and character and look especially for people who have customers in common with you. Teach your fellow club members about your business and learn about their businesses.

L ila, owner of a decorating franchise, and Dean, a home remodeler met at a trade show, then got to know each other better volunteering their time to fix up a house for a low-income family. They began to refer business to each other and decided to expand their lead potential by inviting a deck builder, a pool and spa company owner, and a real estate agent to meet with them every other Friday morning for breakfast. As trust grew in this "customer common" group, they all began carrying each other's brochures and business cards. *"About 20 percent of my business is coming from my referral club,"* reports Lila.

*U*se your Agenda in your conversations. Will you really miss talking about the weather or the ball scores?

46

Leverage Your Layover

When you have a layover in the middle of your flight, have some names and phone numbers of contacts to call in that city. Be ready to tell a success story when the person you've called asks that inevitable question, *"What's new?"* If the person you are calling isn't available, leave a well-planned, positive message. *"I'll call you next month when I'm back in town. I remember how your son loves the Washington Redskins. I got an autograph for him, and I'll send it to you as soon as I get back to the office."*

*A*s president of the local chapter of her professional association, Jane decided a good way to follow up on her association contacts was to talk with presidents in other cities. When she had a two-hour layover in Atlanta, she took along Sheila's name and number. She reminded Shelia that they'd met at a nationwide leadership training meeting earlier in the year. Even though Shelia couldn't talk long, she and Jane made an appointment for breakfast at the upcoming national convention.

*I*n a networking encounter, make
sure you listen at least half the time.

47

Park and Walk

Park your car in a new spot in the parking lot every day and walk into work with a different contact every day.

*G*etting out of her car one morning, Carmen noticed a woman struggling to carry an unwieldy stack of posters and charts into the building. Carmen offered to help, and the women introduced themselves. Carmen found out that Nancy's company sub-contracted the kind of technical training she needed for a proposal she was working on. Later, Carmen told Nancy, *"I'd looked at the name of your company on the building directory a million times and always wondered, 'What do they do?'"* They scheduled an appointment, got to know each other, and eventually bid on several jobs together.

T ake every opportunity to tell the people you meet about your contacts' expertise and successes.

48

Pick Up Donations

Enlist your contact in an easy volunteer effort — collecting hotel soaps and shampoos for a battered women's shelter, for example. Offer to come by and collect what your contact has to donate. People who are called to help say donating something makes them "feel good — and feel good about the person who is organizing the effort."

*A*nn's 17-year-old daughter was set director for the high school's spring play. The crew needed paint for the sets, but it wasn't in the budget. At a networking meeting, Ann stood up and announced, *"If you're cleaning out your garage and have any partly used cans of latex paint sitting around, I'll gladly come by and pick them up."* She later explained, *"I know that informal and repeated contact gives networking relationships a chance to develop. I had a chance to talk with each person who donated paint. And, I've noticed that they all remember me and come up to chat at meetings now. That probably wouldn't have happened if I'd just handed them a business card."*

Y ou can't buy a network.
Paying your dues does
not create a network.

49

Take an Active Role

Serve on a committee, task force, or board. Choose your involvement carefully. Remember, you're placing a very important person (yourself) in a very important position. Build your reputation as a do-er. Pick a job that allows you to exhibit your expertise and show off your talents. Get to know the group before you agree to any job, so that you place your expertise where it can be used best and where you will shine.

*G*ary, a creativity consultant whose business involves bringing more humor into the workplace, was asked to join the Humane Society's board. He offered to emcee the annual awards banquet and introduce the keynote speaker, the director of the zoo. He vowed he'd make that introduction fun and unforgettable. Working out the details with the speaker ahead of time, Gary showed up at the dinner in a gorilla suit, grabbed the microphone and proceeded to give a very serious history of the speaker's accomplishments, and then sat down — ON not at — the head table, where he looked adoringly at the zoo director, nodded his approval during the speech, and led the applause afterward.

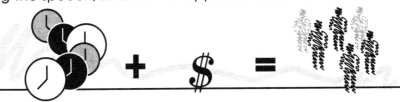

K nowledge is power. Each networking contact expands your knowledge base because you have access to everything and everyone that person knows.

50

Interview Your Contact

Interview your contact for a speech or article you are writing. Most people appreciate the exposure. Be sure to include your contact's credentials or business name in the article or speech and look for other ways to use the publicity to open up opportunities for your contact. If you aren't a writer or speaker, find people who are and pass your contact's name (with his or her permission) along to them as a resource.

*E*llen met the author of a book on franchising at a booksigning at her favorite book store. Soon afterward, she called and asked if he'd be willing to be interviewed for the career resources newsletter she produced at the military base where her husband was stationed. In the course of her short telephone interview with the author, Ellen mentioned that her husband was about to retire and that they were thinking of buying a franchise. He invited them to the local meeting of franchisors and suppliers — a group she might not ever have found if she hadn't followed up with him.

Your networking contacts are part of your sales force — and you are part of theirs.

51

Get Fit

Meet a contact for a walk or jog, using
your fitness time for networking.

Jeff met Bob when they took a training class together. Later that week, Jeff remembered that they had something in common — as over-45 fathers of new babies, they had both remarked that they were concerned about wanting to get — and stay — in shape. So, Jeff called Bob and suggested they meet at the health club a couple of mornings a week to work out.

When your contact gives you a lead or referral, complete the circle. Let your contact know the good things that happened when you got in touch with that lead or referral.

52

Celebrate

Take time to smell the roses. When you're successful, celebrate. Find an excuse for a party — a new office, the anniversary of your business, a new contract, completion of a project. Look outside your business for reasons, too. You might kick off the football season or celebrate a winning team or entertain a visiting guru.

I *'m planning to have a Flood's Over celebration,"* Sharyn says. *"My business wasn't damaged by the flood, but since we're located near the area that flooded, I want to make sure people know that we are open. I'll send the party invitations to all my regular customers, as well as potential customers."*

*U*se your ingenuity.

Your Way

Tell us about a technique that you have used successfully to re-connect, follow up, and stay in touch. If you'd like to tell us about several ways, please photocopy this page.

Your Name _____

Address _____

_____

Phone (work) _____

Phone (home) _____

Mail to
Waymon & Associates
622 Ritchie Ave.
Silver Spring, MD 20910
(301) 589-8633

Or call
1-800-352-2939

Anne and Lynne's Agenda

We are always looking for organizations that would like to
- schedule a keynote speech on networking for a meeting.
- schedule a workshop on networking.
- buy books in bulk (10+).
- develop a strategic plan for Relationship Management.

If you know of an organization that would like what we have to offer, let us know.

Name of Organization _____

Contact _____

Address _____

_____

Phone _____

Mail to

    Waymon & Associates
    622 Ritchie Ave.
    Silver Spring, MD 20910
    (301) 589-8633

Or call us at 1-800-352-2939

Your Name _____

Your Phone _____

About the Authors

Co-authors of **Great Connections: Small Talk and Networking for Businesspeople,** Anne Baber and Lynne Waymon are the nation's experts on business networking.

Their articles on networking have appeared in Delta Air Lines' SKY Magazine, The National Business Employment Weekly, American Express's Your Company Magazine, Entrepreneurial Woman, and many other publications.

Baber and Waymon are sisters and professional speakers. They provide workshops and keynotes to corporations, associations, and professional groups on how to make the most of networking opportunities. They offer training and one-on-one coaching for people who depend on networking for business and career success — entrepreneurs, sales professionals, people in professional services, owners of franchises, independent agents, and those in career transitions.

Waymon also gives seminars on negotiation skills, the power of influence as a personal and organizational tool, and on career development.

Baber also gives seminars on business writing for managers and for PR, corporate communications, and marketing communication staffs.

Their third book, **"Fireproof" Your Career: Survival Strategies for Volatile Times**, will be published by Berkley in 1995. Both Anne and Lynne present workshops on career management, using the strategies in their books.

To Order

Qty.	Titles	Price	Total
	Great Connections: Small Talk and Networking for Businesspeople Paperback Hardback	$11.95 $24.95	
	52 Ways To Re-connect, Follow Up, & Stay In Touch . . . When You Don't Have Time To Network	$14.95	
	Networking for the Home-Based Business Person (60-min. live video)	$49.95	
	Network Your Way To the Job You Want (60 min. live audiotape)	$12.00	
	SUBTOTAL Maryland residents add 5% sales tax		
	Postage/Handling $3 for first item and $1 for each additional item Additional items _____ x $1 =		$3.00
	TOTAL ENCLOSED		

Make your check to Waymon & Associates;
Mail to:

Waymon & Associates
622 Ritchie Ave.
Silver Spring, MD 20910

Or call us (301) 589-8633 or 1-800-352-2939.